Addison Wesley

Science & Technology 6

Life Systems

•

Diversity of Living Things

Steve Campbell   Jim Wiese

Douglas Hayhoe   Beverley Williams

Doug Herridge   Ricki Wortzman

Lionel Sandner

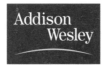

Addison Wesley

Toronto

Coordinating & Developmental Editors
Jenny Armstrong
Lee Geller
Lynne Gulliver

Editors	**Researchers**
Susan Berg	Paulee Kestin
Jackie Dulson	Louise MacKenzie
Christy Hayhoe	Karen Taylor
Sarah Mawson	Wendy Yano, Colborne Communications Centre
Mary Reeve	
Keltie Thomas	

Consultants
Nora Alexander, Valley View Elementary, Durham Board of Education
Ann Clark, Ontario Agricultural College, University of Guelph
Lynn Lemieux, Sir Alexander MacKenzie Sr. P.S., Toronto District School Board
Sidney McKay, Brookbanks Education Centre, Toronto District School Board
Klaus Richter, formerly Edgewood P.S., Toronto District School Board

Pearson Education Canada would like to thank the teachers and consultants
who reviewed and field-tested this material.

Design
Pronk&Associates

ISBN 0–201–64991–8

This book contains recycled product and is acid free.
Printed and bound in Canada.

6 – TCP – 05

Diversity of Living Things

Everything on Earth can be divided into two groups: living and non-living. What do you think determines if something is living? What special qualities or characteristics do living things have?

Believe it or not, you share Earth with about 1.5 million different types of living things: plants and animals. And those are just the ones we know about. Scientists think there may be millions more that haven't been identified yet. Get ready to discover and classify or group the amazing variety of living things on planet Earth!

Now you will find out:

- ways that classification systems can be used around your home, school, and community

- how classification systems help us study the diversity of plants and animals

- how plants and animals are classified to help us identify them

Diversity at the Zoo

Get Started

Every day you see a **diversity** or variety of living things in your life. If you look around your classroom you will see and hear your classmates, your teacher, and maybe even a classroom pet like a hamster. If you look out a window you will probably see trees, birds, weeds, or flowers. Of course, what you see depends on the time of year and even the time of day.

How can you keep track of all these living things?

One of the best places to observe diversity is at the zoo. Look at the **organisms** on these pages. "Organism" is just another word for "living thing." How can you arrange these organisms into groups in a way that makes sense to you? Share your ideas with your classmates.

Work On It

1. Work with a partner. On sheets of paper, list all of the non-living things you notice at the zoo. How do you know they are non-living?

2. On sheets of paper, list all of the living things you notice at the zoo. How do you know they are living?

3. Divide the living things or organisms on your list into two groups. Label each group. Identify and record one characteristic that is shared by *all* the organisms in each group.

4. Identify and record one characteristic for each organism that is shared by only a *few* other organisms in the group.

5. Use the characteristics you have just identified in Step 4. Divide each group of living things into two or three subgroups. Make sure you record the reason for each subgroup.

6. Use a large sheet of chart paper to display all the groups you have made. Make sure you include the characteristics you used to group the living things.

Communicate

Write

1. Post your completed work on a wall along with your classmates' work. Look at your classmates' work.

2. Describe some of the different ways your classmates organized the living things. Count how many different ways the living things were grouped. Which way seems most helpful? Why?

3. Start a mind map to record the new scientific words you will learn in this unit. Begin with the word "living things" in the centre. What new scientific words can you add to your mind map? Keep adding to your mind map throughout this unit.

1 Methods of Classifying

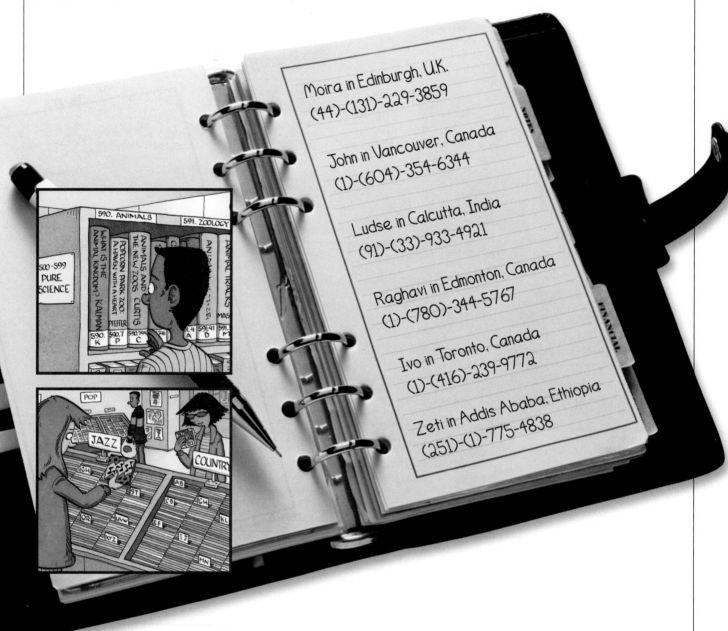

Get Started

After looking at one another's work in the last activity, you saw that there are many different ways of classifying living things. Non-living things can also be classified. With a partner, determine how the illustrations of non-living things shown here have been classified.

There are many other ways of classifying things. One common method is called the "tree classification" system. This system can be used to classify many things, not only trees!

A tree classification system looks a little like an upside-down tree. That's where the name for this system comes from. The chart and explanation below show how it works.

- The top level of the tree contains the general name that covers everything you want to classify. In this case, we want to classify where people live. Our general name is "The World," since everybody lives somewhere in the world.

- The second level divides the general name into groups. In our example, "The World" is divided into continents—Antarctica, Europe, Australia, North America, South America, Asia, and Africa.

- The third level divides each group into subgroups. Here, each continent is divided into specific countries. Note that not all countries are shown in the example.

- Finally, each country can be divided into provinces, territories, or states. This example shows how a tree classification system identifies the Province of New Brunswick. Note that not all provinces and territories are shown in the example.

- There can be as many levels as you want in a classification tree. Each level divides the groups in the level above into smaller subgroups.

Use the tree classification system. Copy this chart. Add to the chart the extra levels needed to show the actual location of the different houses you and your classmates live in.

Where in the World Do You Live?

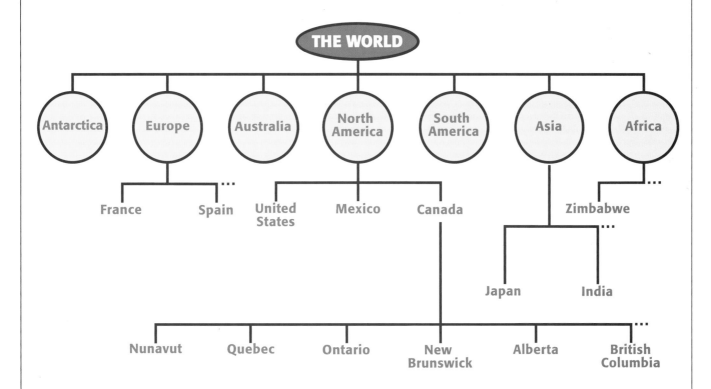

Communicate

Write Present

1. Design a tree classification system to classify these transportation vehicles.

   a. Can you think of a good name for the top level of your tree?

   b. Organize the vehicles into two, three, or four groups. Label each group. Use these labels as the second level of your tree.

   c. Divide your groups into subgroups. Label each subgroup. Use these labels as the third level of your tree.

   d. Continue making as many levels as needed, until each transportation vehicle is in its own group.

   e. Do your groups and subgroups make sense? Have a classmate try it out. Modify or change your tree if necessary.

   f. Present your tree to your classmates and explain how it works.

2. What other things could be classified using the tree classification system?

2 Classifying Living Things

Humans have lungs to breathe with.
Worms are usually pink, brown, or black.
Frogs can live in water and on land.
Plants die when it gets very cold.
Flowers are pretty.
Tigers are striped.
Birds have wings.
Grasshoppers can jump high.
Trees have roots.
Spiders like to eat flies.
Elephants give birth to live young.

Get Started

You have now explored different ways of classifying both living and non-living things. Using the tree classification system, you showed that where you live in the world is different from where your classmates live. That same system could be used for anyone, anywhere on Earth. Such a system is useful when we need to figure out what something is or where it belongs. Plants and animals can also be classified.

What characteristics do you think can be used to classify plants and animals? Look closely at the list of characteristics given above. Which ones would be most useful for classifying plants and animals? Which ones would not? Sort the list into these two groups.

The Five Kingdoms

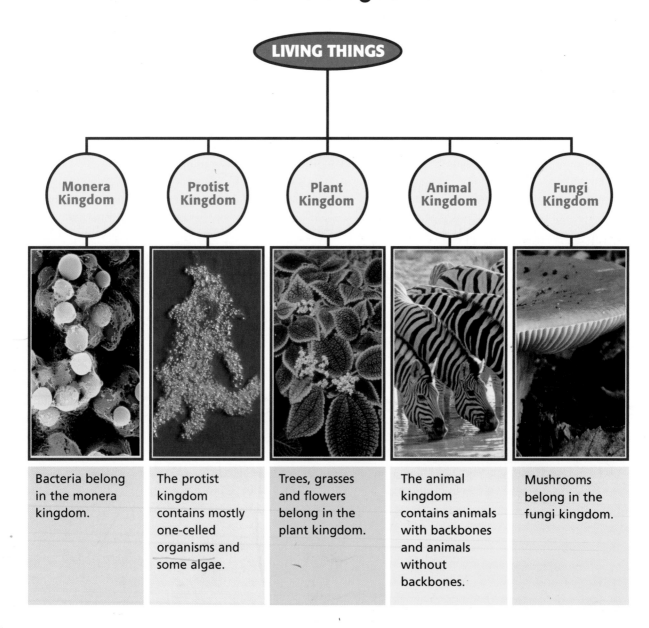

LIVING THINGS

Monera Kingdom	Protist Kingdom	Plant Kingdom	Animal Kingdom	Fungi Kingdom
Bacteria belong in the monera kingdom.	The protist kingdom contains mostly one-celled organisms and some algae.	Trees, grasses and flowers belong in the plant kingdom.	The animal kingdom contains animals with backbones and animals without backbones.	Mushrooms belong in the fungi kingdom.

Work On It

There are different ways of classifying living things. Most classification systems organize plants, animals, and other living things into five large groups called **kingdoms**. This is an evolving or changing system as scientists discover more about the world of living things.

We will now take a closer look at three of these kingdoms: the plant kingdom, the animal kingdom, and the fungi kingdom. On the next page are some of the main characteristics of these kingdoms:

Name of Kingdom	Characteristics
Plants	make their own food, don't move around
Animals	get their own food from eating other organisms, move around
Fungi	obtain food from other organisms, don't move around

Use the organisms in the illustration from the activity, **Diversity at the Zoo**. Put each living thing or organism into one of these three kingdoms. If you don't know where to put some living things, create another group labelled "Not sure."

If Time Allows

Continue your tree classification chart for the organisms you have just grouped. The first level should be labelled "Living Things" and the second level "Plants," "Animals," and "Fungi." Divide these three kingdoms into subgroups.

Communicate

Discuss Write

1. You divided the 11 characteristics from the beginning of this activity into two groups. Which groups would be most useful for classifying plants and animals? Why?

2. Name the five kingdoms of living things.

3. Why are fungi not like plants or animals?

Build On What You Know

You are going to build a classification tree chart for living and non-living things in your life. It will be called *My Tree*. Start the chart with your name and your picture at the top. Create two groups—living and non-living things in your life—as the second level. Under the living things group, create three subgroups of living things in your life as the third level. Similarly, under the non-living things group, create three subgroups of non-living things in your life.

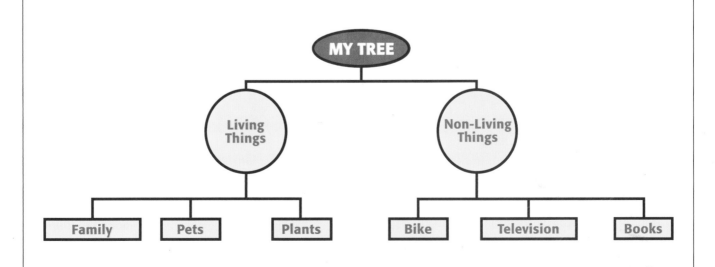

3 Classifying Trees

Get Started

There are over 270 000 different plants known on Earth, and scientists are discovering more each day. This is where a common classification method is useful. Classification is important for scientists all over the world to communicate using the same special words or terms.

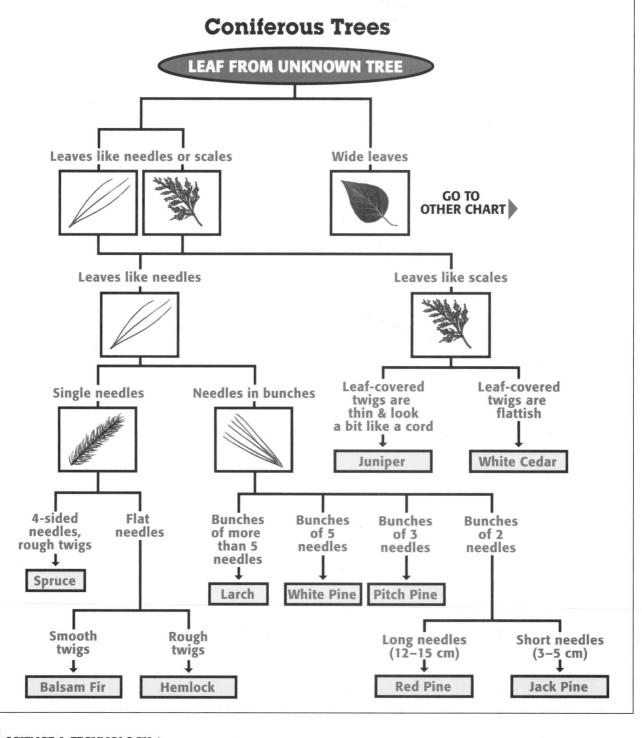

Coniferous Trees

LEAF FROM UNKNOWN TREE

Leaves like needles or scales

Wide leaves — GO TO OTHER CHART ▶

Leaves like needles

Leaves like scales

Single needles

Needles in bunches

Leaf-covered twigs are thin & look a bit like a cord → **Juniper**

Leaf-covered twigs are flattish → **White Cedar**

4-sided needles, rough twigs → **Spruce**

Flat needles

Bunches of more than 5 needles → **Larch**

Bunches of 5 needles → **White Pine**

Bunches of 3 needles → **Pitch Pine**

Bunches of 2 needles

Smooth twigs → **Balsam Fir**

Rough twigs → **Hemlock**

Long needles (12–15 cm) → **Red Pine**

Short needles (3–5 cm) → **Jack Pine**

Deciduous Trees

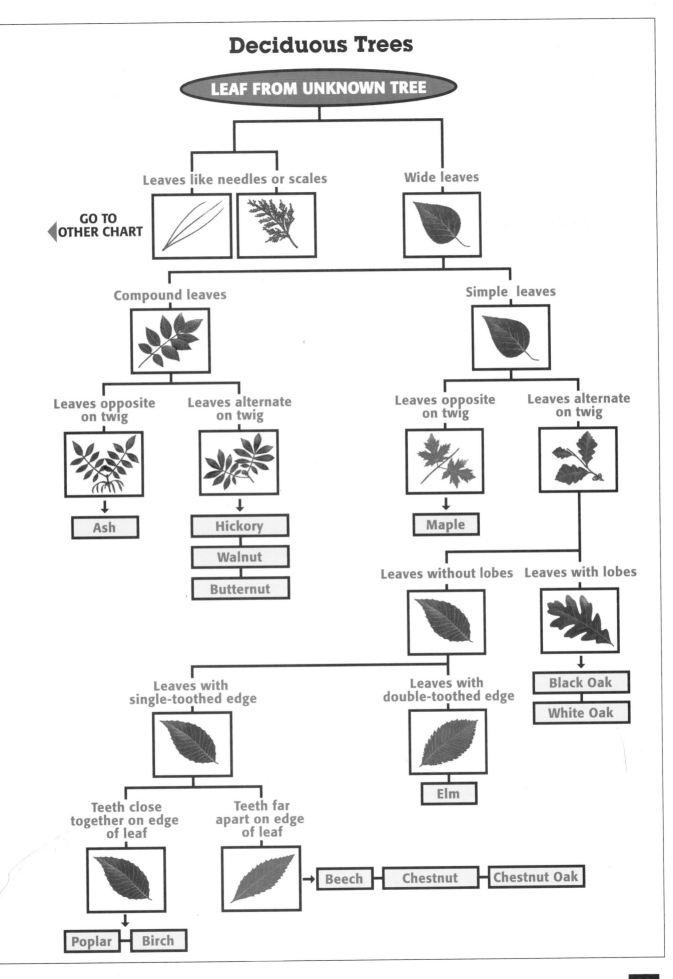

LEAF FROM UNKNOWN TREE

Leaves like needles or scales

GO TO OTHER CHART

Wide leaves

Compound leaves

Simple leaves

Leaves opposite on twig → **Ash**

Leaves alternate on twig → **Hickory** / **Walnut** / **Butternut**

Leaves opposite on twig → **Maple**

Leaves alternate on twig

Leaves without lobes

Leaves with lobes → **Black Oak** / **White Oak**

Leaves with single-toothed edge

Leaves with double-toothed edge → **Elm**

Teeth close together on edge of leaf → **Poplar** — **Birch**

Teeth far apart on edge of leaf → **Beech** — **Chestnut** — **Chestnut Oak**

Canada has many different types of trees. In fact, there are probably several different types or **species** of trees growing in your school yard or neighbourhood. Now it's time to identify some of the trees in your area.

Procedure

1 On the previous pages is a tree classification chart.

2 Use the classification chart to identify these leaves:

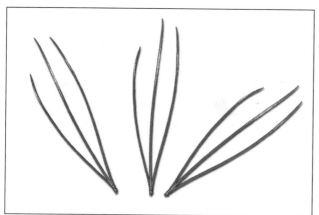

3 You will study trees in your school yard to observe the leaves on the branches. These are your samples. Do not pull the leaves off the branches. The position of the leaf on the branch is important when identifying a tree.

4 Work with a partner to identify the unknown samples.

Communicate

Write

1. List the trees you and your partner identified.

2. If you identified one of your samples as being Walnut, Hickory, or Butternut, how can you find out which of the three types of trees you have?

3. Are there any leaves or needles you collected that could not be identified? Why do you think you were unable to identify what you collected?

4. Use your own words. Describe the difference between a **deciduous** and a **coniferous** tree.

5. Add any new scientific words you have learned to the mind map you started at the beginning of this unit.

Build On What You Know

Add three different kinds of plants to your *My Tree* chart. You might need to add one or more subgroups to your chart in order to classify them.

4 Classifying Animals—
The Invertebrates

Invertebrates in the Animal Kingdom

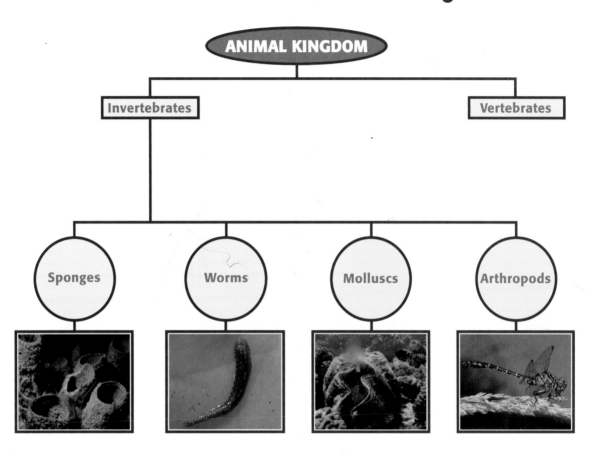

ANIMAL KINGDOM

Invertebrates   Vertebrates

Sponges   Worms   Molluscs   Arthropods

Get Started

The animal kingdom has a wide diversity of living things. It is common to group animals into two categories: animals without backbones, called **invertebrates**, and animals with backbones, called **vertebrates.**

You may be familiar with many different kinds of invertebrates. For example, butterflies, spiders, worms, clams, snails, and slugs are all invertebrates. Each of these animals belongs to a different subgroup. You are going to develop a classification system that will allow you to identify and describe the characteristics of some common invertebrates.

You will create a tree classification system that allows you to place each invertebrate within a subgroup.

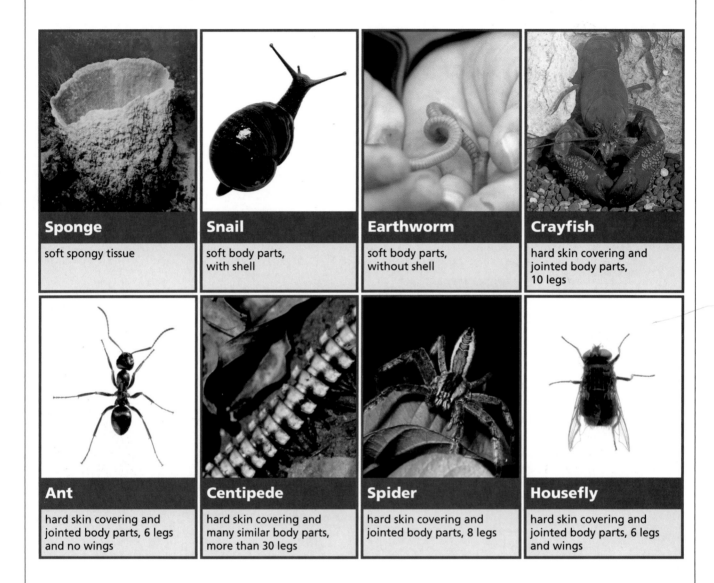

Sponge

soft spongy tissue

Snail

soft body parts, with shell

Earthworm

soft body parts, without shell

Crayfish

hard skin covering and jointed body parts, 10 legs

Ant

hard skin covering and jointed body parts, 6 legs and no wings

Centipede

hard skin covering and many similar body parts, more than 30 legs

Spider

hard skin covering and jointed body parts, 8 legs

Housefly

hard skin covering and jointed body parts, 6 legs and wings

Procedure

1 Use the photos given here. Classify these invertebrates into two groups. Use the characteristics for each animal as clues.

2 Label each group with the characteristic shared by the animals in the group.

3 Now take each group and divide it into subgroups. Continue until each invertebrate is in its own subgroup. Label each subgroup.

4 Classify each invertebrate on this page by placing it in one of the sponge, worm, mollusc, or arthropod groups. Research any additional information needed in the library or on the Internet.

Insects Help Police Solve Crimes

Sometimes police have to solve a crime without many clues. This is often the situation when police investigate a murder. One of the most important pieces of information police need is the time of death. If there are no witnesses, this can be very hard to determine.

By studying the insects on a dead person's body, scientists called forensic entomologists can discover the time of death. Gail Anderson of Simon Fraser University in Vancouver, British Columbia, is one of the world's expert forensic entomologists. If police can't figure out when a person was murdered, they ask Gail to help. Gail checks out the murder scene with the police. Then she attends the victim's autopsy, the medical examination that decides on the cause of death. Gail collects insects from the victim's body and analyzes them. She studies them with a microscope and identifies them with a classification key.

Gail says the insects develop on a dead body at a predictable rate. For example, blowflies—the insects most commonly found on dead people—lay their eggs within minutes of death. "You can look at the insects on the body and figure out how long they have been there. So if they have been on the body for two months, then the person has been dead at least two months," Gail explains.

Grasshopper

Scorpion

Moth

Flatworm

Sponge

Communicate
Write

1. Where can you add the animals shown to your invertebrate classification tree?

2. Look at the photos of the invertebrates you classified. What other characteristics could you use to help you make your tree classification?

3. Can you name any characteristics that would not be helpful to you?

4. Record any questions you would like to ask Gail Anderson.

5. Would you like to be a forensic entomologist? Why or why not?

Build On What You Know

Think of an animal you didn't know was an invertebrate before you started this activity. Add it to your *My Tree* chart.

5 Classifying Arthropods

Of all the invertebrate groups, arthropods contain the greatest diversity of animals. Arthropods include lobsters, millipedes, centipedes, spiders, crabs, scorpions, shrimp, and insects. Arthropods are found in more habitats in the world than any other animal group. Their huge variety of **adaptations** is what has made them so successful in different habitats. Adaptations are special features that help living things survive in different habitats. The adaptations outlined on this page are shared by all arthropods.

- hard outer body covering called an **exoskeleton** (for example, a beetle)

- specialized mouth parts (for example, the **proboscis** of a mosquito that sucks its victim's blood)

- jointed legs (for example, a spider's legs)

- compound eyes (for example, the eyes of a fly)

- segmented body (for example, a centipede)

TREE OF LIFE #3

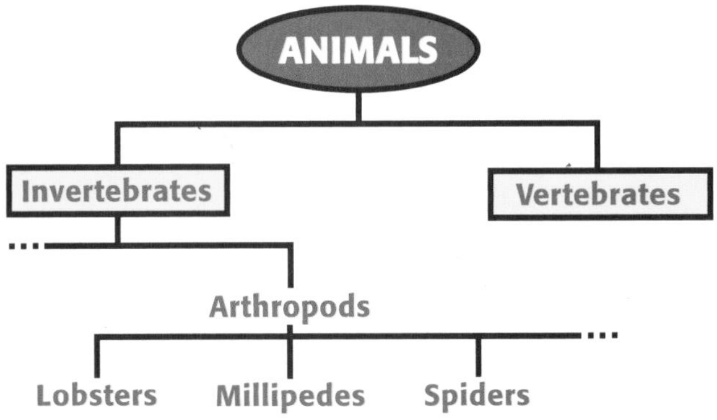

ANIMALS
Invertebrates
Vertebrates
Arthropods
Lobsters
Millipedes
Spiders

TREE OF LIFE #4

ARTHROPODS
Spiders
Lobsters
Insects
Ants
Bees
Mosquitoes

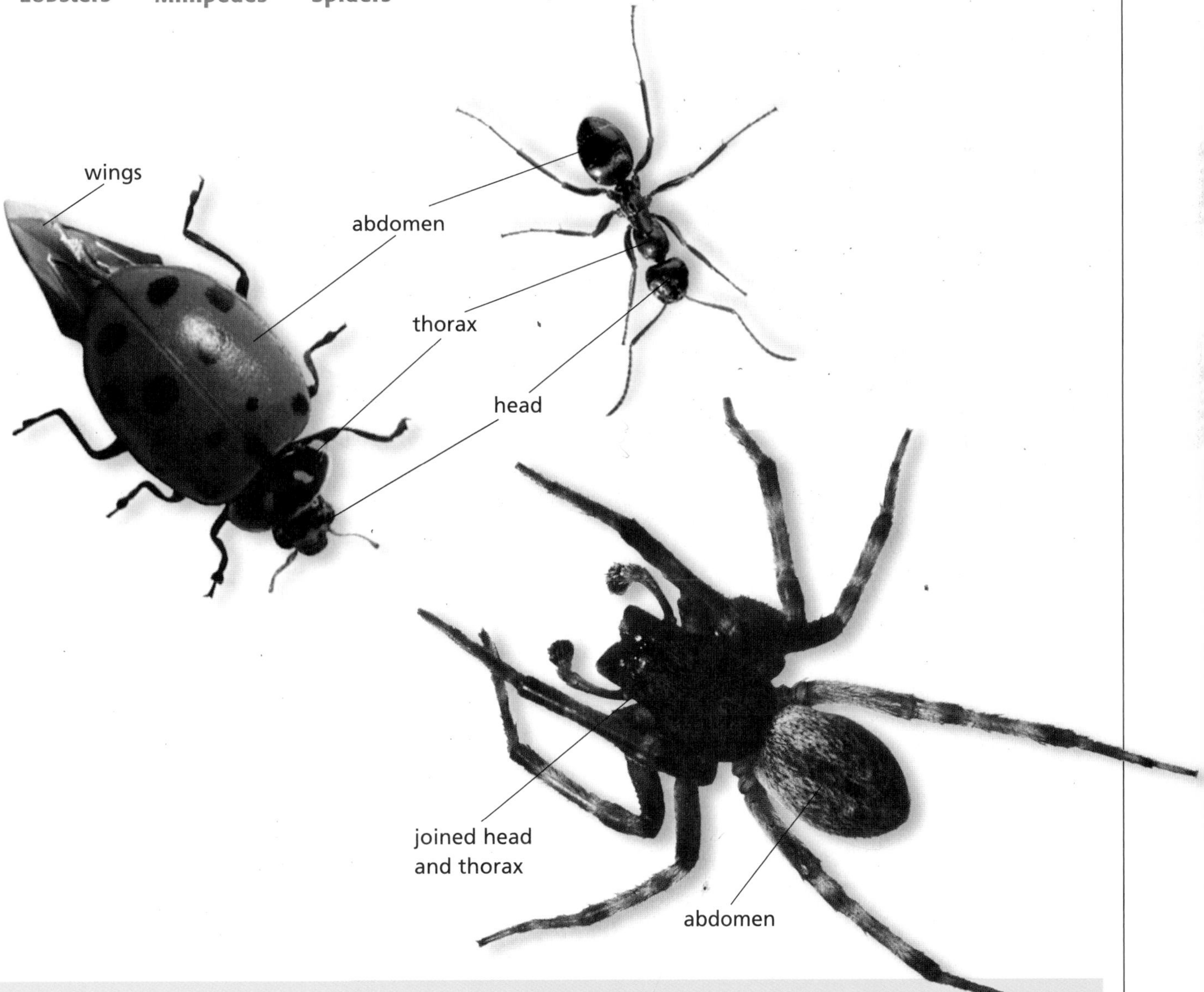

wings
abdomen
thorax
head
joined head
and thorax
abdomen

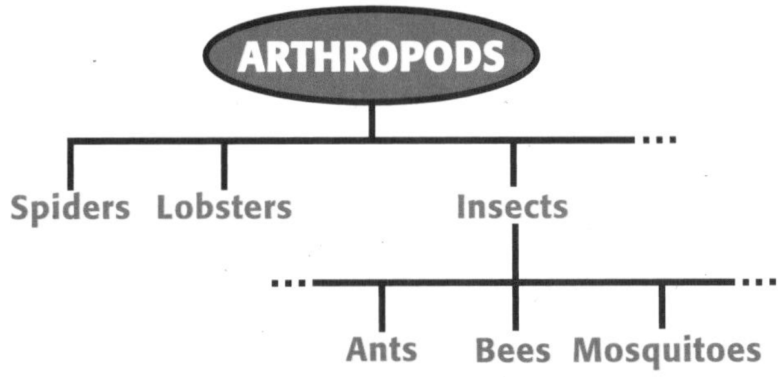

Although spiders and insects are classified as arthropods, they belong to different subgroups of arthropods. People often confuse spiders with insects. Insects have three main body parts: a head, a **thorax** (the second section of an insect's body), and an **abdomen** (the third section of an insect's body). Insects also have six legs and up to four wings which come out of the thorax. But spiders have two body parts—a joined head and thorax, and an abdomen—and eight legs.

Now that you know the basic characteristics of arthropods, it is time to examine the variety of this invertebrate group. Use **specimens** or samples your teacher provides, or the photos below. Identify the similarities and differences among these animals. Record your observations.

Choose a pet you are familiar with, and one of the arthropods from the photos below. Create a poster that shows the similarities and differences between the two animals you have chosen.

Grasshopper

Beetles

Ant

Crab

Butterfly

Wasps

Communicate
Write

1. What are two characteristics shared by all the arthropods you have studied?

2. Name some characteristics that describe only one of the arthropods you have studied.

3. Which of the following characteristics are more helpful for classifying arthropods? Give an explanation for each of your answers.
   - jointed legs
   - three main body parts
   - rough skin
   - colourful wings
   - tiny size

4. Create an information poster on either one of the arthropods you have studied or another one you know about. Your poster should include information on where it lives, what it eats, how long it lives, and its life cycle. Remember to include diagrams, if necessary.

5. Add any new scientific words you have learned to the mind map you started at the beginning of this unit.

6 Observing an Arthropod— The Mealworm

Get set to meet the mealworms! They're a living group of arthropods. These squiggly, yellow creatures are the "babies" of the insect called the Darkling or Grain Beetle. At this stage of their life they are called **larvae**. After about three to five months larvae **moult**, or shed their shells, several times before they develop into **pupae**. The pupae don't eat or move. The insect parts are rebuilt inside the pupae. This takes about two weeks until the skins of the pupae split open and the adult beetles crawl out.

Mealworms like to live in quiet, undisturbed areas. Like all animals, they need to eat to get energy for their bodies. A little bit of food can keep a mealworm alive for a long time. Mealworms have special body parts, or **structures**, that are adapted to help them eat.

Work On It

In this activity, you will investigate mealworms. Your job is to observe the mealworms, describe how their mouthparts work, and investigate a question you have about mealworms.

How Do Mealworms Eat?

Materials for each group:

community of mealworms in a breathable container

magnifying lenses

dry cereal

blank white paper

lined paper

pencils

Optional Materials:

blunt tweezers   plastic gloves

Procedure

1 Carefully place a mealworm on a blank sheet of white paper. Make sure you do not squeeze too hard if you are using tweezers.

2 Use the magnifying lens to observe the mealworm.

3 Draw a diagram of its structure. Label the three parts of its body—head, thorax, and abdomen—and any other body parts you know.

4 Put a few flakes of the dry cereal next to the mealworm. Observe how the mealworm's mouthparts work to allow it to eat. Record your observations.

5 Describe how you think the mealworm's mouth is adapted to eating the cereal and other foods.

Safety Caution

Always wash your hands after handling animals, plants, or soils.

Finding Out More About Mealworms

Materials for each group:

community of mealworms in a breathable container (from previous activity)

any other materials you may need

Procedure

1 With your group, think of a question about mealworms that you would like to investigate.

2 Plan an investigation to find out the answer to your question. Make sure your investigation will not hurt the mealworms. In order for your investigation to be a **fair test**, all the **variables** must be the same or controlled, except one. How will you make sure your test is fair?

3 How will you measure what happens during your investigation? What will the measurements tell you about the variable you are testing?

4 Record and discuss your results with your group. How will you organize and present your results so that your classmates will understand them?

Communicate   Write   Discuss   Present

1. Present the results of your investigation to the class. Discuss each group's question and results.

2. How could you modify or change your question to get more useful results?

3. Consult some reference material and see what you can find out about the mealworm's life cycle. Does it eat different foods at different times during its life cycle? Record your findings.

Build On What You Know

Add at least three examples of arthropods to your *My Tree* chart. Try to pick arthropods you have seen outside the school. Can you create two different subgroups for these animals?

7 Classifying Animals— The Vertebrates

TREE OF LIFE #5

Vertebrates in the Animal Kingdom

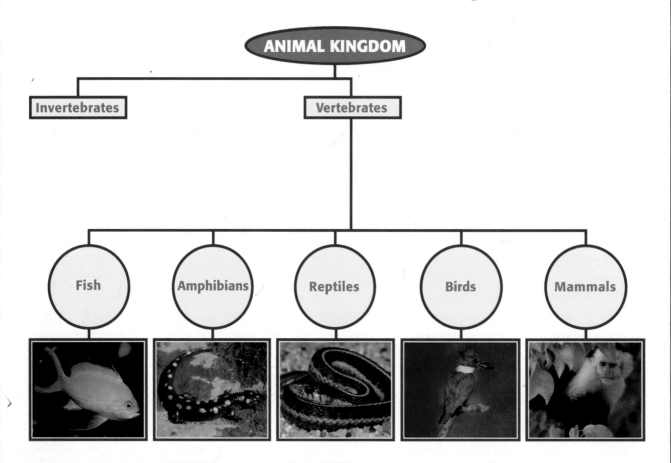

ANIMAL KINGDOM

Invertebrates | Vertebrates

Fish | Amphibians | Reptiles | Birds | Mammals

Get Started

Now that you know about animals without a backbone, what about those with a backbone? Animals with a backbone are called vertebrates. Touch your own backbone. How do you think your backbone helps you? Scientists put all vertebrates together into one group in the animal kingdom. Then they divide the vertebrates into five major subgroups: fish, amphibians, reptiles, birds, and mammals.

Characteristics of Vertebrates

Fish, amphibians, and reptiles are **cold-blooded** animals. This means that the temperature of their body is the same as that of their surrounding environment. Cold-blooded animals do not use a lot of energy to keep the inside of their bodies warm.

Birds and mammals are **warm-blooded** animals. This means that their body temperature is maintained at a particular temperature, no matter where they are. Warm-blooded animals use a lot of energy to keep their bodies warm. Warm-blooded animals can live in very cold climates, where cold-blooded animals would not survive. Do you know why this is so? Did you know that you are a mammal? All humans are part of the mammal subgroup of vertebrates. Humans are warm-blooded. At what temperature is the human body maintained? How can you find out?

Here are some examples of the different types of vertebrates, along with some characteristics of each subgroup:

Characteristics of Fish

- most have bodies covered with scales
- cold-blooded
- breathe through gills
- most lay eggs

Examples shown here:

- angel fish and skeleton
- cod
- shark

Characteristics of Amphibians

- soft, moist skin
- four legs (often with webbed feet)
- cold-blooded
- most lay eggs

Examples shown here:

- frog and skeleton
- salamander
- newt

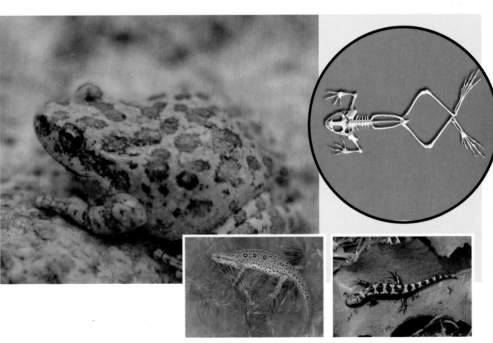

Characteristics of Reptiles

- dry skin covered with hard overlapping scales
- most have four legs
- cold-blooded
- most lay eggs

Examples shown here:

- lizard and skeleton
- snake
- turtle

Characteristics of Birds

- feathers
- a beak or a bill for a mouth and no teeth
- warm-blooded
- breathe through lungs

Examples shown here:

- pigeon and skeleton
- hummingbird
- robin

Characteristics of Mammals

- all have hair at some stage in development
- warm-blooded
- breathe through lungs
- mothers nurse their young

Examples shown here:

- human and skeleton
- dog
- giraffe

Work On It

Work with a partner. Research one animal from each group of vertebrates. Use a variety of reference materials to find out how each of these animals has the same characteristics as its group. Organize your information in the following categories:

- Body shape and description
- Body temperature: warm- or cold-blooded
- How it breathes
- How it reproduces
- Any adaptations that help the animal survive in its habitat
- How it feeds

When scientists classify living things, they must use **structural characteristics**. These characteristics stay the same throughout the life of a living thing. Also, they are shared by all the members of the species.

In animals, some structural characteristics are:

- bone structure (or lack of bone structure)
- the circulatory system
- the reproductive system

In plants, some structural characteristics are:

- seed production
- ways of transporting minerals and nutrients inside the plant
- root systems

Structural characteristics are easily recognized in living things, so they can be used by scientists all over the world.

Communicate Discuss Write

1. Compare your research with that of your classmates. Discuss the similarities and differences you found in animals that belong to the same subgroup of vertebrates.

2. Create a chart to show the five subgroups of vertebrates. Use your classmates' research to list as many animals as you can that belong in each subgroup.

3. Humans are vertebrates. In what subgroup do we belong?

4. Add any new scientific words you have learned to the mind map you started at the beginning of this unit.

5. Explain why you think scientists use structural characteristics and not physical appearance to classify vertebrates.

6. The Arctic and deep-sea hot vents are two examples of habitats with extreme conditions. What adaptations are needed by the organisms that live there? What would happen to the organisms if these habitats did not exist?

Build On What You Know

Add an animal from each vertebrate subgroup to your *My Tree* chart. Pick vertebrates you would like to have as a pet, or to observe outdoors.

8 All About Fish

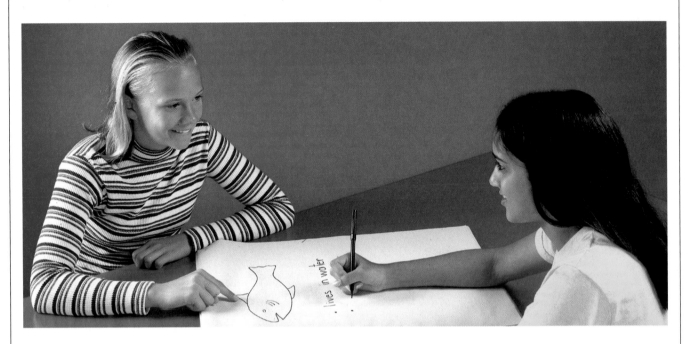

Get Started

In the last activity you learned about some of the characteristics of vertebrates—fish, amphibians, reptiles, birds, and mammals. Without looking back at the last activity, brainstorm with a partner everything you know about fish. Make a list. Compare your list with other classmates. Modify or change it, if necessary.

Work On It

In this activity, you will observe a fish to find out how it is adapted to life in its habitat (water). Like all vertebrates, fish have a backbone that runs along the middle of their body. This backbone is made of either cartilage or bone, and it is flexible.

Materials for each group:

large, clear container (big enough so a fish can swim freely)

goldfish or other small fish

small net   water

pencils   paper

Procedure

1. Work with your group. Fill the large container with water that has the same temperature as the water holding the fish.

2. Use the net to transfer one fish into the large container.

3. Carefully observe the fish for 15 min. Make notes and diagrams on how the fish moves and breathes.

continue...

4 How does the fish breathe?

5 Why do you think the fish's eyes are located where they are? Is this helpful or not? Explain.

6 How many fins can you spot on the fish? What do you think the different fins do?

7 With your group, discuss and record any questions you have about the shape of the fish's body and its movement.

8 Make a list of any other observations or questions your group has about the fish and how well it is adapted to living in its habitat.

9 When you have finished observing your fish, put it back in the aquarium.

10 Work with your group. Look at your observations. Discuss how the following characteristics help a fish survive:

- body covered with scales
- fins
- breathing through gills
- no neck

Communicate   Write   Discuss

1. Research in the library or on the Internet. Draw a diagram of a fish like the one you just observed. Label the different body parts and make notes in point form to explain how these body parts help the fish move and survive.

2. Name some habitats near your home or school where you would expect fish to live.

3. **a.** Some fish habitats are being threatened by human activity. With the class, discuss what would happen to the fish population if the habitats for fish disappeared or became extremely polluted.

   b. Create a poster to show the importance of maintaining clean and healthy habitats for fish and other living things.

4. Add any new scientific words you have learned to the mind map you started at the beginning of this unit.

5. Compare the characteristics of vertebrates and invertebrates. How are they the same? different? Use a chart, table, or graph to display your results.

If Time Allows

Even though they live in water, whales are mammals, not fish. Research to find out if you can determine why whales are mammals and not fish.

A Prehistoric Vertebrate

Get Started

About 225 to 64 million years ago there were many different kinds of living things roaming Earth. Dinosaurs during that time were the controlling or ruling animal. As you may know, these animals no longer exist on Earth. Even though they have disappeared, they remain a fascinating subject for many people. Today, scientists called **paleontologists** study dinosaurs and other forms of life that existed long ago.

How can paleontologists figure out what organisms were around that long ago? One way is to study **fossils**—the traces and bones of plants and animals that lived long ago. A dinosaur fossil is usually the hardened remains of a bone or tooth. Sometimes other parts of a dinosaur, like its scaly skin, can also be preserved.

Velociraptor roamed Earth about 100 million years ago. This **carnivorous** dinosaur was about 1.8 m long and hunted in groups. Scientists think *Velociraptor* was speedy and intelligent. These characteristics made it a good hunter. The fossil in the left corner helped reconstruct the skeleton of *Velociraptor.*

Work On It

Paleontologists carefully collect fossils and put them together to build or reconstruct the skeletons of dinosaurs. They then use the reconstructions to help explain the dinosaurs' characteristics. Get ready to become a junior paleontologist!

Your job is to study a fossil and compare it to some animals that are alive today. Find similarities or differences between the fossil and the animals that exist now. Start by checking out the recently found fossil of *Velociraptor* you see here.

Procedure

1 Look closely at *Velociraptor* seen here. Then take a good look at the skeletal diagrams of the fish, bird, cat, and dog on the next page. What are the similarities and differences between *Velociraptor* and each of these four animals?

2 Make a list of all these similarities and differences.

3 Share and compare your findings with your classmates.

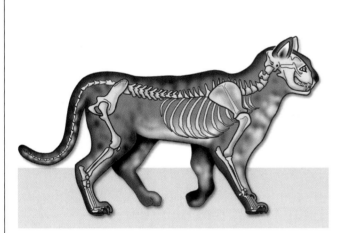

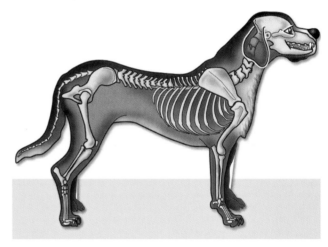

Communicate

Write

1. Which animal seen here do you think is a descendant of *Velociraptor*? Explain why you think so. How can you check your answer?

2. What can fossils tell scientists about animals that are alive today? Explain.

3. Add any new scientific words you have learned to the mind map you started at the beginning of this unit.

If Time Allows

Look carefully at the pictures of *Velociraptor*. Make a list of any special adaptations you can see, such as its claws. How do you think each of these adaptations helped *Velociraptor* to survive in its habitat? What do you think its habitat was like? If you don't know, how can you find out?

 # 10 The Key to Classifying

Get Started

You have now had many opportunities to classify plants and animals. In each situation you used characteristics of the animal or plant to classify it. For example, a pitch pine tree has thin needles in bundles of three. A snail has soft body parts with a shell. Classification usually depends on the external or internal characteristics that are constant for all members of the species.

Living things also have characteristics that are not useful for classifying. Can you think of what some of these might be? Share your ideas with your classmates.

In your class discussion you may have identified characteristics such as size, colour, or behaviour as not useful for classifying. Two types of characteristics that are helpful for studying living things but not for classifying them are **physical appearance** and **learned behaviours**.

Physical Appearance

Look around your classroom. Do all your classmates have the same eye colour? What about hair colour? That is because not everyone looks alike. Although we are all humans, we come in many shapes, sizes, and colours. These differences make everyone unique and special, but are not necessarily useful characteristics for classifying.

Learned Behaviours

You also have other characteristics that people associate with you, such as your ability to talk, read, and play sports or a musical instrument. These abilities are learned. Depending on your environment, you may have different opportunities to learn different skills. Some animals are also able to learn certain behaviours.

Make a list of the kinds of behaviour you have learned.

Physical appearance and learned behaviours are important for scientists when *studying* living things. However, they're not very useful for *classifying* living things. These types of characteristics can change over time, and they are not shared by all members of the species. That is why scientists use structural characteristics to classify living things.

The skills you use to play baseball and the harp are learned behaviours. You can improve these skills with instruction and practice.

Communicate Write

1. What is the difference between physical appearance and learned behaviours? Give an example of each type of characteristic.

2. Why do scientists use structural characteristics to classify living things?

3. Give an example of a structural characteristic shared by all humans.

4. Add any new scientific words you have learned to the mind map you started at the beginning of this unit.

11 The Microscopic World

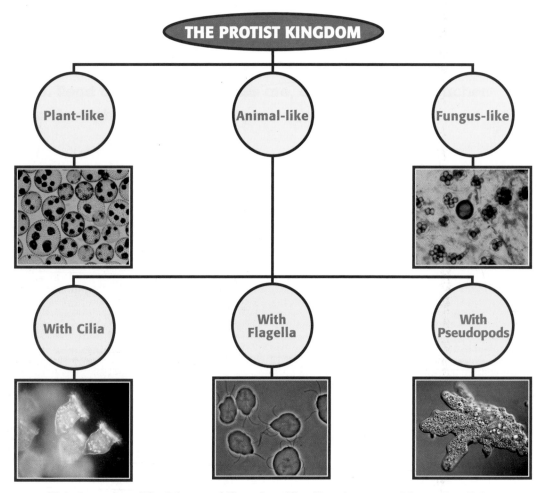

TREE OF LIFE #6

THE PROTIST KINGDOM

Plant-like

Animal-like

Fungus-like

With Cilia

With Flagella

With Pseudopods

This is a simplified form of the classification tree used by scientists.

Get Started

Living things come in all sizes and shapes and live in very different habitats. You are familiar with the living things that you can see. But there is another group of living things that may not be as familiar to you—because they are so small they are invisible to the human eye!

These tiny living things are called **microorganisms**. You need a microscope to see them. Scientists classify microorganisms by their structural characteristics such as internal systems and body structure. You will examine some microorganisms that come from the protist kingdom.

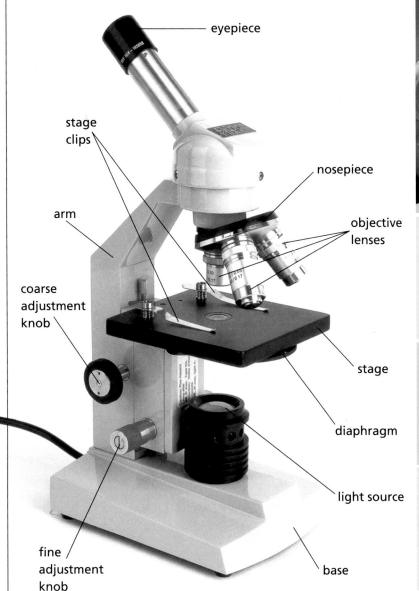

- eyepiece
- stage clips
- arm
- coarse adjustment knob
- fine adjustment knob
- nosepiece
- objective lenses
- stage
- diaphragm
- light source
- base

Cilia, the hair-like projections on the surface of some micro-organisms, are used for movement.

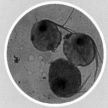

Flagella are long whip-like tails used for movement.

Pseudopods are extensions that look like fingers, and are used for movement or to catch prey.

Work On It

Microorganisms live in soil, water, and many other habitats on Earth. In this activity, you will observe some microorganisms from the protist kingdom. You will find out how they meet their basic needs. The photos on the next two pages are microorganisms from the protist kingdom that you may see on your slides.

What is a basic need? What do you think are your basic needs?

Materials for each group:

living microorganisms in slides or viewing containers

sheets of white paper   pencils

magnifying glass   microscope

Safety Caution

If your microscope uses a mirror, be careful not to reflect direct sunlight into your microscope. You could damage your eyes.

continue...

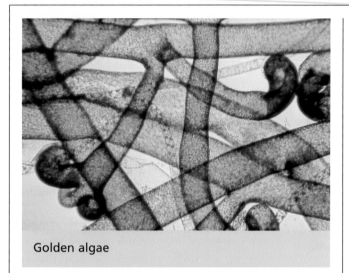

Golden algae

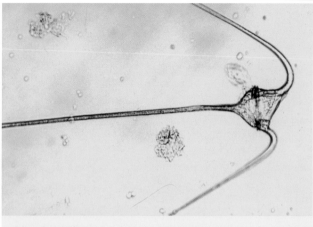

Dinoflagellate

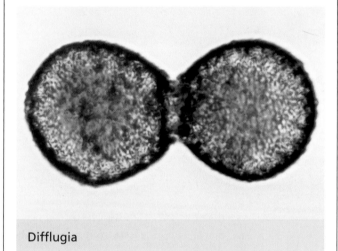

Difflugia

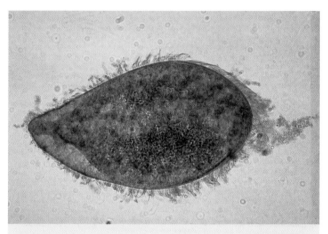

Opalina

Procedure

1 Use a pen to write your name on a piece of paper. Look at your name with the magnifying glass and record your observations. What do you see with the magnifying glass that you couldn't see before?

2 Now place the piece of paper onto the microscope stage. Move the piece of paper gently from side to side and up and down, while looking through the microscope. Notice that when you move the paper one way, it *looks* like it's going in the opposite direction.

3 Practise focussing the microscope.

4 Carefully place one of your slides or viewing containers on the microscope stage. Select the lowest power objective lens and focus it. Make sure you focus slowly so that your microscope lens will not hit the slide.

5 If you want to magnify your image more, select a higher power objective lens.

6 Draw sketches of your observations. Write descriptions in point form of the living things you see.

7 Repeat steps 4 to 6 with any other slides or viewing containers.

8 Work with your group. Discuss your observations. Try to identify different features you observed on the slides.

Vorticella

Diatom

Communicate

Present Discuss Write

1. Share and compare your diagrams and observation notes with those of your classmates in other groups. Do you notice any similarities among the specimens you observed?

2. Are there any basic needs for micro-organisms that you didn't see being met? Work with a group. Research one of the microorganisms you observed. Use the library or the Internet.

   Find out how it:
   • feeds
   • moves
   • breathes
   • gets rid of waste
   • reproduces

   Present your findings to the class. Be creative in your presentation.

3. Add any new scientific words you have learned to the mind map you started at the beginning of this unit.

Build On What You Know

Add at least two microorganisms to your *My Tree* chart. Explain why you chose them.

Classifying Living Things Around Us

Get Started

You've explored classification. Now it's time to try out your new skills and identify plants and animals around a pond, field, or other habitat near your school and then design a classification system for them. Before you go out, let's review what you have learned so far:

- Classification systems are used by people to help them identify plants and animals.

- Classification systems are based on structural characteristics rather than physical appearance (such as eye colour or hair colour) or learned behaviours (such as playing the guitar or learning a second language).

- Some structural characteristics include bone structure for animals and root systems for plants.

Work On It

How many different types of living things do you think you can find in a field, forest, pond, or other habitat near your school? In this activity, you will go on a field trip to collect data on the different types of living things that you can see or find evidence of in a nearby habitat.

Things to Remember:

1. *Noise and activity may scare away some living things.*

2. *Living things may leave an environment when there is a disturbance. They will return after the disturbance is gone.*

3. *Different pieces of evidence like nests, broken nutshells, feathers, and animal tracks can give clues as to what living things inhabited the area.*

4. *Do not disturb the environment by collecting or removing anything from it.*

On a Field Trip

Materials for each pair:

recording material (paper, pencil, camera, video recorder)

magnifying lens

popsicle sticks

guide or classification chart for local plants and animals

the Trees Classification Chart from the **Classifying Trees** Activity (optional)

Procedure

1 Decide on the boundaries for your field trip observations.

2 When you arrive at the observation area, choose an individual location and sit quietly for 5–10 min. Look and listen for signs of living things.

3 Make a list of the different living things you observe. If you know the name of any of these living things, write it down.

4 Sketch and describe the plants and animals you see. Try to include as many details as you can.

5 Use the guide for local plants and animals to help you identify some of the living things you observe. If you have the Trees Chart with you, use it to identify the trees.

6 With your partner, examine the ground in your observation area with a magnifying glass. Use the popsicle stick to carefully move some of the plant material aside so you can observe the top layer of the soil.

7 Move to a new area and continue to add to your list.

Safety Caution

Always wash your hands after handling animals, plants, or soils.

Back in Class

Materials for each pair:

chart paper   a pen or marker

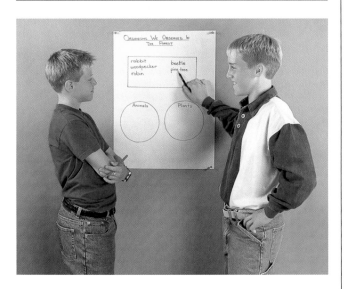

Procedure

1 With your partner, look at your list and classify the living things you observed. Plan your classification system by dividing the living things into two groups: Animals and Plants. If you observed fungi, make a third group called Fungi.

2 Within these two or three groups, divide the living things into subgroups. Try to use the subgroups for plants and animals that you learned in this unit. Remember that members of a subgroup should share at least one characteristic. Label each subgroup.

3 Share your list of groups and subgroups with a few of your classmates. Combine your lists on the chart paper, and organize the groups and subgroups again as you did in steps 1 and 2.

4 Draw a diagram to show the classification system your group designed for the living things you observed.

5 Make a table that lists the different types of living things you found on your field trip.

6 Does your classification system make sense? If not, make any necessary changes.

Communicate
Write Present Discuss

1. Present your classification system to the class and explain how it works.

2. What type of characteristics did you and your partner use to create your subgroups? How did this help you classify the living things?

3. When you shared your list with a few of your classmates, were your subgroups within the animal and plant kingdoms similar or different?

4. What reasons did your classmates give for their classification system? If your subgroups were different, how did you resolve your differences when you combined your lists?

5. Think of five living things in your area that you did not observe on the field trip. How could they be added to your classification system?

Review

Demonstrate What You Know

Get Started

Now it's time to show how much you have learned about diversity of living things. Read over what your tasks are, and talk to your teacher if you are unclear about what to do.

Flatworm   Turtle   Shield bug

Nautilus   Goose   Frog   Salmon

Work On It

Your job is to classify the 18 living things you see here. When you have finished, each of the 18 living things should be in a subgroup on its own.

As you divide the living things into groups and subgroups, you must identify the characteristics you used.

This will help others understand why the living things are in the different subgroups you have chosen. Try to use the subgroups you have already learned in this unit.

You may choose your own way of presenting your classification system, but it must clearly show the characteristics and the members of each subgroup.

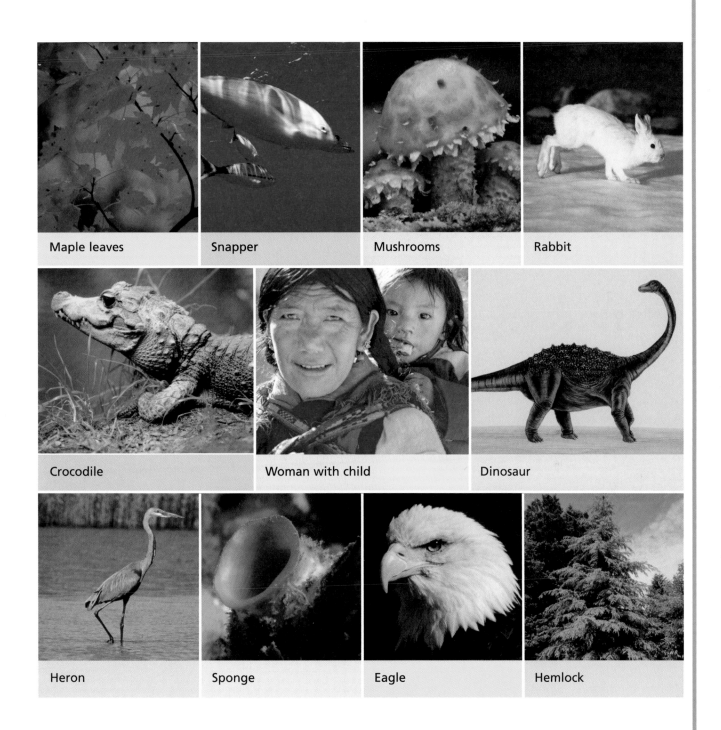

Maple leaves   Snapper   Mushrooms   Rabbit

Crocodile   Woman with child   Dinosaur

Heron   Sponge   Eagle   Hemlock

Now check your work.

☑ My classification system classifies each living thing.

☑ My classification system uses structural characteristics to classify living things.

☑ My presentation clearly shows the characteristics I used to classify the living things.

☑ My classification system can be used by a classmate or someone outside the school.

Review

Communicate

Now it's time to think about how well you did. Use this chart to help you score your work. Four stars is the highest score for each.

1 Star ★

2 Stars ★★

3 Stars ★★★

4 Stars ★★★★

- How much do you know about classification? Look at the classification system you designed. Does your work show you know

A little about classification	Some information about classification	A lot of information about classification	All about classification?

- Look at the characteristics you used in your work. Does your work show you have applied

A few of the structural characteristics	Some of the structural characteristics	Most of the structural characteristics	All of the structural characteristics?

- Now look again at your classification system. Will it be clear and precise to a reader?

Not very clear or precise	Somewhat clear and precise	Mostly clear and precise	Very clear and precise

- Now look at how you've presented your classification system. Can a classmate or someone outside the school be able to follow it? Do you think it shows

Not much understanding	Some understanding	A good understanding	A complete understanding?

Explain Your Stuff

What did you learn about diversity of living things?

1. What kinds of characteristics are used for scientific classification systems? Why are these kinds of characteristics used?

2. Describe some of the ways scientific classification systems can be helpful.

3. Name three different organisms that live in your neighbourhood. What adaptations do they have that help them survive in this particular habitat and in other places?

4. How are a snake and an earthworm similar? How are they different? Use some of the scientific words you've learned in this unit to explain your answer.

5. What is the main difference between warm- and cold-blooded animals? How does being warm-blooded or cold-blooded affect the life style of that animal?

6. Why is someone's ability to play basketball not a useful characteristic for classifying that person scientifically? What is a useful characteristic for classifying humans?

7. How does this fossil help us understand the ways in which animals change over time?

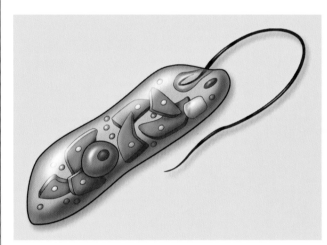

8. Describe the microorganism above in detail. Include any information you think would be helpful in classifying the microorganism.

9. Put all the "Tree of Life" diagrams provided in this unit (there are six in total) together to create one big "Tree of Life."

Review

How Did You Do?

1. List three things that you didn't know before this unit started.

2. Describe what you liked best in this unit.

3. Give yourself a pat on the back! What did you do well in this unit?

4. List three questions you still have about diversity of living things.

Now you know a lot about diversity of living things! Here are some of the things you have learned:

- There are a variety of classification systems in the world for everything from music and books to plants and animals. The tree classification system is a common way to classify both living and non-living things.

- Scientific classification systems for animals are based on structural characteristics rather than physical appearance or learned behaviours.

- Classification keys can be used to identify plants, animals, and microorganisms.

- Invertebrates are a diverse range of animals without backbones.

- Arthropods are one group of invertebrates that show a wide range of diversity, from shrimp to mealworms and grasshoppers.

- Vertebrates are animals with backbones.

- Vertebrates have specific adaptations that allow them to live in different habitats.

- Fossils can be used to study similarities and differences among animals that lived long ago and animals that are alive today.

- Fossils can tell us a lot about the changes in animals over time.

- When scientists find a fossil, they need to interpret clues to identify it.

- All microorganisms meet their basic needs of food, air, water, and movement in various ways.

Glossary

abdomen the third section of an insect's body

adaptations special features, like fur or webbed feet, that help a living thing survive in its habitat

arthropods a diverse group of invertebrates that have characteristics such as jointed legs and hard outer covering of their bodies (exoskeleton)

carnivorous eating animals or animal parts

cilia hair-like projections found on the surface of some microorganisms. They are used for movement.

cold-blooded a term used to describe vertebrates whose body temperature is the same as that of the water or other habitat they're living in

coniferous cone-bearing; most evergreen "needle"-trees are coniferous

deciduous falling off or shedding at a particular season, or stage in growth

diversity variety

exoskeleton hard outer covering of the bodies of arthropods

fair test an investigation carried out under controlled conditions. In a fair test, all variables are controlled except the one under investigation.

flagella the long whip-like tails found on some microorganisms. They are used for movement.

fossils the traces and bones of things that lived long ago

invertebrate an animal without a backbone

kingdom a large group used in classifying living things. There are five kingdoms: monera, protist, plant, animal, and fungi.

larva (plural **larvae**) the immature form of an insect that hatches from an egg

learned behaviours characteristics that are learned, such as the ability to play the piano or ride a bicycle that are not useful for classifying living things

microorganisms living things too small to be viewed by the human eye

monera kingdom the kingdom containing bacteria and blue-green algae

moult to shed the outer skin or an exoskeleton, or other outer layers such as hair and feathers

organisms living things

paleontologist a scientist who studies forms of life that existed long ago

physical appearance characteristics such as size, shape, and colour that are not useful for classifying living things

proboscis the tube-like mouthparts of some insects

protist kingdom the kingdom containing many different types of microorganisms such as amoebas and paramecium

pseudopods extensions that look like fingers, used by some microorganisms for movement or to catch prey

pupa (plural **pupae**) the resting stage in an insect's life cycle that occurs between the larva stage and the adult insect

species a specific type of organism

specimens samples used for study of experiments

structures specialized body parts

structural characteristics characteristics that are constant for all members of the species and will not change over time

thorax the second section of an insect's body

variable anything in an investigation that can be changed

vertebrate an animal that has a backbone

warm-blooded a term referring to vertebrates whose body temperature is maintained at a particular temperature, no matter where they live

Acknowledgments

The publisher wishes to thank the following sources for photographs, illustrations, articles, and other materials used in this book. Care has been taken to determine and locate ownership of copyrighted material used in this text. We will gladly receive information enabling us to rectify any errors or omissions in credits.

Photography

p. 1 (centre) PhotoDisc, Inc., p. 1 (bottom) PhotoDisc, Inc., p. 4 PhotoDisc, Inc., p. 6 (photos from top left) Corel Stock Photo Library, Corel Stock Photo Library, PhotoDisc, Inc., Corel Stock Photo Library, PhotoDisc, Inc., Corel Stock Photo Library, Corel Stock Photo Library, Mike Timo/Tony Stone Images, Corel Stock Photo Library, PhotoDisc, Inc., Corel Stock Photo Library, Corel Stock Photo Library, Dennis O'Clair/Tony Stone Images, Lorne Resnick/Tony Stone Images, p. 8 (photos 1–5 from left) S. Lowry/Univ. Ulster/Tony Stone Images, Cabisco/VISUALS UNLIMITED, Corel Stock Photo Library, Corel Stock Photo Library, Corel Stock Photo Library, p. 13 (photos 1–4 from left) Corel Stock Photo Library, Ivy Images, Corel Stock Photo Library, Corel Stock Photo Library, p. 14 (photos 1–8 from top left) Corel Stock Photo Library, G. K. & Vikki Hart/The Image Bank, Sue Ann Miller/Tony Stone Images, Kelvin Aitken/First Light, Charles Krebs/Tony Stone Images, Corel Stock Photo Library, Corel Stock Photo Library, James Cotier/Tony Stone Images, p. 15 (photos from top left) (photos 1–3, 5) Corel Stock Photo Library, (photo #4) T.E Adams/VISUALS UNLIMITED, p. 16 (photos 1–5 from top left) (photos 1, 2, 5) Corel Stock Photo Library, (photo #3) PhotoDisc, Inc., (photo #4) Jim Zuckerman/First Light, p. 17 (top) Charles Krebs/Tony Stone Images, p. 17 (centre & bottom) PhotoDisc, Inc., p. 18 (photos 1–6 from top left) (photos 1–2) Corel Stock Photo Library, (photo # 3) Gary Vesta/Tony Stone Images, (photos 4–6) Corel Stock Photo Library, p. 19 Ivy Images, p. 20 Ray Boudreau, p. 21 Ray Boudreau, p. 22 (photos 1–5 from left to right) Corel Stock Photo Library, p. 23 (top left) Corel Stock Photo Library, p. 23 (top right) John D. Cunningham/VISUALS UNLIMITED, p. 23 (top left inset) Corel Stock Photo Library, p. 23 (top right inset) Corel Stock Photo Library, p. 23 (bottom left) Corel Stock Photo Library, p. 23 (bottom right) Gilbert Twiasi/VISUALS UNLIMITED, p. 23 (bottom left inset) Ivy Images, p. 23 (bottom right inset) Corel Stock Photo Library, p. 24 (top left) Corel Stock Photo Library, p. 24 (top right) John D. Cunningham/VISUALS UNLIMITED, p. 24 (top left inset) PhotoDisc, Inc., p. 24 (top right inset) Corel Stock Photo Library, p. 24 (bottom left) Corel Stock Photo Library, p. 24 (bottom right) Don W. Fawcett/VISUALS UNLIMITED, p. 24 (bottom left inset) Corel Stock Photo Library, p. 24 (bottom right inset) Corel Stock Photo Library, p. 25 (top left) Andy Sacks/Tony Stone Images, p. 25 (top right) PhotoDisc, Inc., p. 25 (centre left inset) Corel Stock Photo Library, p. 25 (centre right inset) Corel Stock Photo Library, p. 25 (bottom) Ray Boudreau, p. 26 (top) Corel Stock Photo Library, p. 26 (bottom) Whol, K. Crane/VISUALS UNLIMITED, p. 27 Ray Boudreau, p. 30 (top inset) Mick Ellison/American Museum of Natural History, p. 32 RBS/First Light, p. 33 (top) David Young Wolff/Tony Stone Images, p. 33 (bottom) Andy Sacks/Tony Stone Images, p. 34 (top left & right) John D. Cunningham/VISUALS UNLIMITED, p. 34 (bottom left) T.E. Adams/VISUALS UNLIMITED, p. 34 (bottom centre) VISUALS UNLIMITED, p. 34 (bottom right) Mike Abbey/VISUALS UNLIMITED, p. 35 (left) Dave Starrett, p. 35 (top) Ray Boudreau, p. 35 (microscopic fields 1–3) M. Abbey/VISUALS UNLIMITED, Arthur M. Siegelman/VISUALS UNLIMITED, Robert Brons/BPS/TONY STONE IMAGES, p. 36 (top left) T.E Adams/VISUALS UNLIMITED, p. 36 (top right) A.M Siegelman/VISUALS UNLIMITED, p. 36 (bottom left) Cabisco/VISUALS UNLIMITED. p. 36 (bottom right) Stan Elems/VISUALS UNLIMITED, p. 37 (left) Cabisco/VISUALS UNLIMITED, p. 37 (right) NHMPL/Tony Stone Images, p. 38 Corel Stock Photo Library, p. 39 (left) Corel Stock Photo Library, p. 39 (right) PhotoDisc, Inc., p. 40 Ray Boudreau, p. 41 Ray Boudreau, p. 42 (top left) John D. Cunningham/VISUALS UNLIMITED, p. 42 (top centre) Corel Stock Photo Library, p. 42 (top right) Corel Stock Photo Library, p. 42 (bottom left) Marc Chamberlain/Tony Stone Images, p. 42 (bottom #2) Corel Stock Photo Library, p. 42 (bottom #3) Tom Ulrich/Tony Stone Images, p. 42 (bottom right) Gary Vesta/Tony Stone Images, p. 43 (photo #2 from top left) PhotoDisc, Inc., p. 43 (all others) Corel Stock Photo Library, p. 45 (top) Spectrum Stock/Ivy Images

Illustration

Steve Attoe: pp. 2–3, p. 4, p. 28
Ted Nasmith: pp. 10–12, p. 29 (dinosaurs), p. 30
Cynthia Watada: p. 29 (map), p. 31, p. 45

Cover Photograph

Artbase Inc.